The Precious Attributes of a Christian Woman

Lee R. McMurrin, Ph.D.

Copyright © 2017 Lee R. McMurrin

Distributed by IngramSpark. This book is also available on Amazon.com.

All rights reserved. No part of this book may be reproduced, stored in a retrieval system, or transmitted in any form, or by any means, electronic, mechanical, photocopying, recording or otherwise; without prior written permission of the author.

Cover and book design by Thomas Osborne
Cover photograph: iStock.com/Antonel

Library of Congress Control Number: 2017905035

ISBN: 978-0-692-86190-5

Printed in the United States of America

DEDICATION

This book is dedicated to my two daughters, Michelle Park and Marianne McMurrin. Each of them helped with the development of the stories that were unique about their mother, Frances McMurrin. Marianne McMurrin made the greatest contribution by editing the manuscript, taking some of the pictures and coordinating all of the photographs with the script of the book.

ACKNOWLEDGEMENTS

Jonathan Park, my son-in-law, greatly enhanced the book by carefully selecting Bible verses for each chapter. Several individuals who were members of the organization known as Visiting Angels, not only provided household services but also took dictation and typed some of the script for this book. The greatest contribution was provided through the professional work of Louise Hawker, who was involved at every step, from the beginning to the publishing of the book. Louise added background information, edited the manuscript, arranged the pictures, and sought out Thomas Osborne. He took the copy of the book and prepared it for publication.

LEE R. MCMURRIN

ABOUT THE COVER

Peonies are known over the years in several countries to be a symbol of honor brought to a family, in this case, it symbolizes "the precious attributes of a Christian woman."

Contents

CHAPTER 1
Introduction, 1

CHAPTER 2
A Committed Christian, 3

CHAPTER 3
Creative and Artistic, 9

CHAPTER 4
Cute Behavior Traits and a Unique Way of Thinking, 25

CHAPTER 5
A Beautiful Lady, 31

CHAPTER 6
Very Intelligent and Bright, 37

CHAPTER 7
Born in a One Room Cabin to Become a World Traveler, 45

CHAPTER 8
Providing Hospitality, 59

CHAPTER 9
A Sincere Spiritual Life Growing Toward Maturity, 65

CHAPTER 1

Introduction

"A wife of noble character who can find? She is worth far more than rubies. Her husband has full confidence in her and lacks nothing of value."

PROVERBS 31: 10-11

My dear wife, Frances McMurrin, lived to be 71 years old and died from the effects of breast cancer after fighting the disease for seven years with 100 injections and 10 chemicals. What I remember most of all are her very special traits and characteristics, as revealed in her rich life experiences. These I have written as Precious Attributes of a Christian Woman, believing this will be helpful to other women as they face challenges in their lives. Men can relate to having a wife who is a Christian and the contributions they make to their families and others they come in contact with.

It has been nine years since Frances went to be with her heavenly Father. Now she is fully experiencing the joys of Heaven. She, through her life and, particularly, during the seven years living with cancer, knew she was well prepared for Heaven. Everyone she came in contact with knew that she was a Child of God. She took the cancer treatments with such grace and patience. In her conversations at the infusion lab, she encouraged the other patients and even the staff.

I wanted so badly to record her many attributes and started writing them soon after the funeral. Those who attended the memorial service would now realize that I used some of these writings to express my thoughts about my precious wife of fifty-one years who was a constant companion and buddy. Frances was gifted and uniquely talented in so many ways that it has been very difficult to finish this writing.

CHAPTER 2

A Committed Christian

"Finally, be strong in the Lord and in his mighty power. Put on the full armor of God, so that you can take your stand against the devil's schemes."
EPHESIANS 6: 10-11

Frances had the gift of prayer. Her prayers were always appropriate and so reverent. I would hear her on the phone praying with a family member or friend and you knew she was connected to the Almighty. She wrote out some prayers that were in her Bibles. She prayed about subjects that were important to her and the lives of others. She prayed for the church, the nation, the world's suffering people and God's Chosen People. She prayed daily for her children and others close to her heart. There was something universal about her prayers that would make them effectual even today.

She had the gift of song and praise. She loved the hymns of the church and would sing them with praise to the Lord while she worked, and at the piano when she had a chance, usually in the evening hours before bedtime. We would wake up in the morning, spending time in bed singing our favorite hymns and songs and playing, "Can you name that tune?"

She had the gift of searching the scriptures. She delighted in the Word of God. Her Bibles are filled with notations on almost every page. She developed a library of reference books on the Bible and Christian theology. If someone raised a question, she would thoughtfully search the Bible and her many references to dig deeply into the subject.

She had the gift of love. She loved her children deeply and missed them when they went off to school. They were always cared for immaculately. She prayed for them and the grandchildren daily, and sometimes over the phone when they called. Her heart of love was overwhelming. The children at church would gather around her and present her with illustrated letters. Large works of art were sent to the home to show their love for her. Love is reciprocal. Her love for the Lord and His Word was seen in her life, and people responded.

Frances was a prayer warrior.

ENDURING AN MRI ORDEAL WITH GRACE

I was taking Frances to the Bend Memorial Clinic for a scheduled MRI. We parked close to the entrance as she was very ill with cancer and I needed to get her into the wheelchair. The oncologist needed to see where, in the body, the cancer was.

When we arrived at the lab, I was told I could not go in with her for the test. So, at 9 a.m., Frances was wheeled into the lab for her test. I was left in the waiting area alone. I checked from time to time with the receptionist. I asked her how my wife was doing. It seemed to me a lot of time was going by and I was concerned. She would reassure me that it would soon be finished. To me, the receptionist appeared very young and inexperienced so I began to doubt her answers. This went on for several hours. I could not understand all the time going by, so I thought maybe she had passed out. She was so sick. I also thought that they had taken her out the side door to the hospital across the street.

Meanwhile, with the passing of time, I found a pamphlet explaining the MRI's procedures. It stated that it took approximately 55 minutes. Then I was really worried for my wife, since many hours had passed.

I remembered during this time that I saw staff members coming out of the lab and passing me in pairs, headed for the concession stand. They were giggling while walking. I thought maybe they were planning a party as they got treats from the concession stand. I did recognize one young lady who bounded by me. My wife and I had seen her in many different offices through the years while my wife was sick. We noticed she didn't stay in one office very long. I felt she was a foolish and giddy young woman. After I reviewed this in my head, I though they were celebrating some event and they left my wife unattended in the tube. At 1:30 p.m., Frances came out of the lab in her wheelchair. She saw by the look on my face that I was worried. She leaned over to me and said, "I don't want to make trouble; I just want to go home." She had gone through enough. She wanted to go home so I took her home.

Later on in the day, she began to open up about the events in the MRI lab. She had been strapped down, and was inside the tube. She didn't see or hear anyone and believed she was left unattended.

After a significant amount of time the machine must have turned off automatically. When that happened, she looked for the emergency button that was hooked to the speaker. The so called "Emergency Button" did not work! The heat from the magnetic coils began to fall down onto her. As if this wasn't enough stress, she realized that the air conditioner also did not work. Frances started to pull her arm free of the strap. When she finally got it out, she began to pound on the side of the tube. She received no answer or help; she began to perspire from all the heat and stress. In all our married life I had never seen my wife sweat. She said she was completely wet.

With no air conditioning and the stifling heat, I believe that sweating may have saved her life. She started forcing herself to relax, as no one was answering her plea. She began to recite The Lord's Prayer and Psalm 23 from the Bible. She did this over and over to keep from panicking. To make matters worse, she needed to use the bathroom. The staff finally returned and she told them to "let her out to use the bathroom." Their answer was, "You need to stay still and finish the procedure." Now at this time she had already spent several hours in that tube.

I felt it necessary, once I learned the terrible details of her ordeal, to send an email to the manager of the lab. He gave me a call after a few days to say that "The machine was new, and we're still learning how it worked." Did I really just hear that kind of excuse coming from a lab with a million dollar machine? I had to think that no one in their right mind would place that machine in a hospital lab and not make sure people were trained to use it. This prompted me to write a letter. I told him, "He was responsible to see the staff properly trained before they used it on people." His next response to me was "The oncologist was responsible because of the many tests he ordered." I had also talked to the doctor and was told by him that two tests were ordered, both common tests. I began to tell the doctor all the details of my wife's ordeal in the MRI machine. I do not know the procedures to file a complaint, but I had told the doctor and the lab manager. I was hoping to hear it got filed.

Another visit to the lab again was ordered by the doctor. When I took Frances to the MRI Lab I noticed there were new lab technicians; two were men. Some changes had been made. This time I was in the room with her. The procedure was on time and done satisfactorily, in my opinion. The results from several tests showed that the cancer had spread to her liver. Frances later died on the 5th of May in 2008.

Many friends felt I should pursue a legal remedy for the MRI ordeal. I was very busy caring for Frances and chose not to follow up with a lawsuit. And now, of course, the main witness was deceased. She survived that ordeal with the testimony of a "Precious Christian Woman." She used her knowledge of the Bible, by repeating the scripture, to keep herself calm. Praying not to have a panic attack or something worse, she put her trust in the Lord, that he would bring her through or that she would be on her way to see her heavenly Father.

CHAPTER 3

Creative and Artistic

"Then, the Lord said to Moses, "See, I have chosen Bezalel, son of Uri, the son of Hur, of the tribe of Judah, and I have filled him with the Spirit of God, with wisdom, with understanding, with knowledge and with all kinds of skills — to make artistic designs for work in gold, silver, and bronze, to cut and set stones, to work in wood, and to engage in all kinds of crafts."

EXODUS 31: 1-5

MAKING CERAMIC DECORATIONS

Frances learned to make ceramic decorations and use a kiln. She decorated Christmas decorations including prized lighted Christmas trees for each of the family members, and a nativity set and other decorations to bring beauty and light to the Christmas season. Some of the first gifts she gave to her mother and other family members were her works of art in ceramics. Frances poured into molds the clay that produced 15 items for the nativity set. She then had to clean them and make sure that they were perfect. Then she had to fire them in the kiln, which she had in the basement. She used her own creative skills to paint each one meticulously. The attention to detail shows up in the eyes of the subjects. The gifts from the three kings were so authentically individualized. She had

to fire the subjects again after painting them. Professional artists said her display of the nativity was the best that they had ever seen.

REPAIRING LEAD GLASS WINDOWS

Frances learned from a highly skilled technician how to repair leaded glass windows. She engaged in leaded glass art, using her tools and skill. She used these same skills to make a Tiffany lamp shade, which decorated our homes. A glass lamp table with a colorful lead glass design of a blooming flower was a valued work of art in our living rooms.

SEWING SKILLS

Sewing projects were extensive. Like her mother who was a seamstress, Frances had a sewing shop with lots of material and all the amenities for sewing. Special gifts were custom-made for the children and grandchildren. Prominent among these were pillows for their bedrooms and colorful maps of North America, which could be hung as tapestries.

VERY CREATIVE DRESSES FOR GRANDDAUGHTER

Frances designed many A-line dresses with a flared skirt for our granddaughter Bethany. Bethany just loved these dresses and modeled them for her mother and house guests. Some of these dresses are still in storage and will become family heirlooms. During her development, Bethany loved to put in her sketch book beautiful ladies in A-line dresses.

DEVELOPMENT OF SEWING ROOM IN BEND, OREGON HOME

Our home in Bend had a building that was used as a shop for the former owner, but was now going to be turned into a sewing room for Frances. Her mother was a professional seamstress who made dresses and suits for the famous elite of Daytona Beach. When she passed away, Frances inherited the many fabrics she had in her home, and brought them to Bend. She may have had 100

Our first sewing machine was an antique Singer which Frances bought at an estate sale.

rolls of fabric, which we donated to a quilting club in Bend. We kept some of it because our daughter, Michelle, still liked to work on projects when she came to visit.

The garage doors in the shop were replaced by sliding glass doors. The shop floor was painted, and shelves were installed to hold the many racks of fabrics.

The sewing room included a center for development of ceramic objects, including a kiln for firing and finishing many ceramic creations. She had the latest computerized sewing machine, which she used to create many fabric maps for each of her children and grandchildren, and other sewing projects. She also had a table supplied and equipped to beautifully wrap presents for birthdays and other celebrations. Incidentally, the sewing room included an antique Singer sewing machine, which Frances found at an estate sale in Milwaukee. The room was also equipped with a television set and a stereo radio. We also had to install a gas heater, in order to keep the sewing room warm during the winter months.

GREETING CARDS A WORK OF ART

Frances was always ready to learn a new type of art. She taught herself calligraphy so she could personalize greeting cards sent on birthdays, anniversaries, and other occasions. Individuals receiving these cards have saved them as classic works of art. They were decorated and included a verse she had either composed or taken from a classical source.

DECORATING SEVERAL HOMES

Frances decorated several homes with curtains and draperies, floor coverings, paint and wallpaper. She learned to decorate the walls with patterned bed sheets, and reupholstered and refinished many pieces of furniture. She had a great sense of color and design, making each home delightful and classically beautiful.

I was moving up the ladder as a school administrator, so we moved a number of times from city to city. Each house we acquired

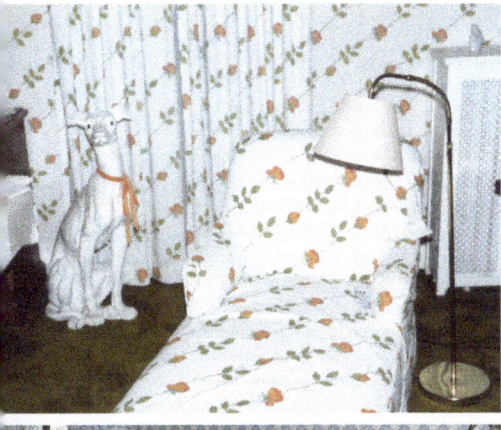

needed improvement. So Frances put her creative talents to work, making each house attractive and comfortable for her family.

OVERSEEING NUMEROUS MOVES

We had various arrangements from moving from one city to the next. Frances was always greatly involved in packing and organizing for each move. In most cases we hired a moving van and had to pack our belongings in boxes furnished to us. However, in one case, the school district paid for the entire move, and the packing of belongings was done by their workers. In this case, Frances did the supervising in the packing, loading and unloading. I helped out as well, of course.

COOKING GOURMET MEALS

Frances was a gourmet cook, with a knack for making very simple meals served with a touch of beauty that could be pictured in a Martha Stewart publication. Frances enjoyed reading and collecting recipes and was willing to try new dishes and desserts she found appealing. As I traveled, I bought books of recipes which were special to that culture and region.

Frances had a good sense of beauty and knew what was valuable. The tree peonies are a good example.

DECORATING OUR YARD

Frances enjoyed working in the yard, cultivating the finest flowers and plants. The tree peonies survived a move from Ohio to the Oregon desert, and were prominent at the front of the house. There they received the attention they needed and bloomed each spring with a gorgeous display of color.

LOOKING BEAUTIFUL

Frances loved to fix her hair and wear wide-brimmed flower laden hats. Once in a great while, she would go to a hairdresser and come home with great dissatisfaction until she redid her hair to fit her sense of beauty. There were no hats that she didn't look like a model in. Hats went out of style but when she wore them she would receive many compliments. Over time, she accumulated many beautiful hats. Several dozen, in fact. In Shaker Heights, Ohio there was a high school with a very active theater program that put on many shows and musicals of days gone by. Frances donated many of her hats to the theatre, which were much appreciated. My daughter Marianne was an assistant principal at Shaker

Heights High School, so there was a personal connection to the school and theatre program. Frances also wore her hats on Easter Sunday, including wearing them to church. And she would receive many compliments when we went out to eat at fine restaurants. She would be the only one in an "Easter bonnet with all the frills upon it."

FINDING A VALUABLE DINING ROOM TABLE

We moved from a house in Toledo, Ohio that had a dining room table built into the wall. Now in Milwaukee we were in a home where we needed a dining room table. Frances was on the hunt to find one, and we were still looking into the Thanksgiving and Christmas season. But on the search around Christmas time she found a table at Goodwill that had been varnished several times and in need of a cleanup. Frances bought the table for $20. They helped her put it on top of the car. She drove all the way home with the table during a snowstorm. After cleaning it up, we found it did have some slight damage. But it also had a beautiful mahogany top and the legs were carved in the famous pineapple legs. It proved to be a very valuable antique. It became a very attractive and valuable table, which we still own today. In Milwaukee, it was placed in a dining room that had oak paneling and stained glass windows. Frances knew how to find a bargain.

Valuable Golden Lamp

THE DISCOVERY OF THE VALUABLE LAMP

There was a very historic, gold, valuable lamp hanging in the circular foyer of the Case mansion in Milwaukee, Wisconsin. The images went back as far as 1589 A.D. We discovered its value and it became a treasured possession in our homes.

Frances upholstered a four-piece sectional sofa, which was more beautiful than the original.

LEARNING TO UPHOLSTER

We had a four-piece living room set, which we purchased soon after we were married. Over the years, with young children, the living room set showed a lot of wear and tear. So Frances took lessons on upholstery and did a beautiful job refinishing the living room set with some very sturdy materials. She upholstered many other pieces of furniture, such as sitting chairs, and antiques which desperately needed upholstering. In Milwaukee, she went to many estate sales. Frances knew how to identify valuable pieces of furniture which could be added to our home. The furniture usually had to be refinished and sometimes repaired.

GROWING SPECIAL PLANTS

Frances liked to have growing plants and flowers in pots throughout the house. These would appear in the living room as well as in the bedrooms. She also contributed to the landscaping by identifying unusual plants and flowers as we would tour greenhouses and flower shops. In Shaker Heights, Ohio she saw a set of unique peonies. Typically, peonies that you find for sale grow from tubers. These were tree peonies, unlike most peonies which die off in the fall and come up with sprouts in the spring. The tree peonies lose their leaves in the fall like a tree, but grow each year and become bushes filled with blossoms each spring. When we moved from Shaker Heights to Bend, Oregon, Frances wanted to bring the tree peonies all the way across the United States to our new home, which was in the desert. The local florist told my wife those plants would most likely die. We planted the peonies in a shady spot next to our home, and they grew into large trees which have been blooming each spring for 16 years now.

FILLING THE YARD WITH GROWING THINGS

We bought a relatively new house in Bend, Oregon. It was on a half-acre lot and had no landscaping at all. So we spent ten-thousand dollars to hire a landscaper to decorate the entire property with trees, shrubs, and grass. Frances worked with the landscaper to beautify the property. Over the years, it has grown to be very attractive and spectacular, adding much value to the property.

LOVED TO COOK

Frances was a gourmet cook, and loved to find recipes to her liking. She would always display the food in the most attractive manner at meal time. She loved to put together meals for the

celebration of birthdays and other events such as Thanksgiving, Christmas, New Years, Easter, and the 4th of July. For these events she liked to get out the best china, silverware, serving dishes, placemats, special napkins, and tablecloths. Her meals were always tasty. She had the unique touch of a Southern cook, and at these events she also specialized in desserts. In several locations we raised strawberries and we would make homemade ice cream. She loved to serve strawberry sundaes.

DECORATIONS FOR HOLIDAYS

Frances made sure that the house was particularly decorated for Christmas, with Christmas trees covered in decorations and lights. She also placed a wreath at the door, as well as evergreen on the staircases and other places in the house. She made special candies for the Christmas season. Peanut brittle was one of her favorites, which everyone loved. She sent out greetings on birthdays, anniversaries and holidays. Frances designed these greetings herself and used her newly developed skill in calligraphy to put script on the cards.

CHAPTER 4

Cute Behavior Traits and a Unique Way of Thinking

"But you are a chosen people, a royal priesthood, a holy nation, God's special possession, that you may declare the praises of him who called you out of darkness into his wonderful light."
1 PETER 2:9

In Milwaukee we had a detached garage with an attic for storage. On a cool day in the spring of the year, she went to the attic to get something important while everyone was at work and at school. The ladder she used fell down and she was stuck for several hours in the attic, rolling up in the awning that covered the sun porch to keep warm. When I came home she had taken out the hexagon window above the garage doors and said in her sweet quiet voice, "Here I am." She didn't scream and yell for help, but managed the situation until I came home from work. After that, when I left home to run errands, I would say with a smile, "Don't go to the attic." Sometimes she would go anyway and tell me that she prayed that the Lord would protect her.

During the winter, in that same driveway, a branch had fallen off the apple tree and I ran over it with the car. She said, in her unique way, "Lee, you knocked out the whole front rear-end."

ATTENDING MY 55-YEAR CLASS REUNION

We both went to my 55-year class reunion at Walbridge, Ohio. The high school was very small and years ago had been consolidated with an adjoining school district. An interstate highway had gone in and the route to the new high school had changed dramatically over this period of time. We finally found a way to get there and were sitting in the parking lot for some time since we were early. We observed people beginning to go into the high school and were about to leave the car when Frances said, "Lee, I think we are at the wrong place. All these people are so old."

Two years ago I was invited to Olivet Nazarene University to be inducted into the Athletic Hall of Fame. My daughter Marianne came to stay with Frances so I could leave to attend this event. When I got home, Frances commented that, "If you were such a good athlete, why did it take 55 years for them to recognize and honor you?" That made sense but that isn't the way the world turns. Again, she had an open and fresh perception of things which wasn't encumbered by tradition or custom or familiar ways of thinking about the world.

RAISING A BOY

Our first two children were girls, and since Frances grew up in a family of girls, she was uneasy about the fact that she was now going to have a baby boy. So she told me, "I don't know how to take care of boys." I told her she would do just fine and that she would learn soon enough.

FRANCES EXPERIENCES FIRST SNOW

Living in southern Georgia and Florida, Frances had not seen snow until we moved to Leetonia, Ohio. Early one Sunday morning we looked out our second story window and it had snowed. I opened the window so she could feel the snow on the window sill. She said, "The snow is so soft and beautiful." On the way to the Methodist Church, which was a block away, the snow fell on her black coat and she thought it looked like diamonds. She was fascinated by it.

Later that week she went on her own to a nearby small city that had a shopping area. When she entered the store it was sunny and clear. When she came out of the store it was dark and had been snowing. Although she had never driven in snow-covered roads before, she started home nonetheless. About halfway home, she ran off the road into a ditch. She walked some distance to a pay phone and called me. I told her that I would be right there to help her and bring her home. She began to cry and said that she would probably have to have her feet amputated since they were frozen. I said, "I know they hurt and they may even feel numb." Then I told her, "No, no, we will slowly warm them up when you get home and you will be ok. They won't have to amputate your feet."

THE PINK BUNNY RABBIT STORY

Frances' granddaughter Bethany was now having her fourth birthday in her home in Renton, Washington. She had to fly from Cleveland to Seattle. Frances knew that Bethany loved stuffed animals; she had a brown stuffed bear that she had nearly worn out. So Frances brought a pink bunny rabbit that was nearly three feet tall to take to Bethany's birthday party. Along the way, she left the pink bunny rabbit on the plane as she exited. It was a funny sight to see a grown woman walking around asking, "Has anyone seen my pink bunny rabbit?" Can you imagine the response she got? She ended up in the baggage claim office and, happily, they were able to deliver the pink bunny rabbit to the Renton address the next day.

MITCHELL WAS A GREAT INFLUENCE

Mitchell was a wonderful black woman who lived in a shack made of throwaway metal with a tin roof and a dirt floor. Because of her relationship with Mitchell in her childhood, she never had the racial prejudice that was common in her immediate environment. Mitchell lived in "colored town" and this was just down the street from where Frances lived in Daytona Beach, Florida. Mitchell had no running water or toilet facilities in her shack. But she came out each morning in a newly starched white dress, ready for work and praising God for his blessings. People would see her coming down the street singing and praising her Lord and would invite her to do some housework. On occasion, she ironed a basket of laundry for Frances' mother, who worked two jobs to keep food on the table. All the time she was ironing, she was proclaiming the promises of God and testifying of His Goodness. Frances often mentioned Mitchell as having a great influence on her young life and her own walk with the Lord.

FRANCES WAS PRONE TO FALLING

Every day, Frances would end her prayers asking the Lord to provide a hedge of protection around her, protecting her from great harm and she put her complete faith in the Lord that he would keep her safe. Although she experienced a number of falls, she survived all of them.

We would be taking a walk to the City Park and Frances would trip and fall, usually landing on the grass rather than the sidewalk. One spring we went to pick blueberries and she stepped on a moss-filled rock and fell. This time she got hurt and had to recover from bruises. While in Shaker Heights, she fell down the staircase and broke her ankle. In this condition she was on crutches. She was very independent about going to the bathroom. I told her I would help her, but she went on her own at night using the crutches, which slipped on the bathroom floor. She fell over the tub and damaged some of her ribs.

While she was in various stages of cancer treatment she fell more than once, usually trying to be independent again and going to the bathroom at night. I always told her I would help her or to use her walker so she wouldn't fall. One night she went on her own to the bathroom and I woke up hearing a thud. I opened the bathroom door and I didn't see her there so I looked around to find her. She was not to be found. So I went into the bathroom, and she was lying flat on her back in the tub with her head on the faucet. She had tried to flush the toilet and fell gracefully backwards into the tub. She didn't get hurt, so I worked to get her out of the tub and back to the bed. On other occasions I had to call the fire department to get her off the floor. She would sometimes fall between davenports and I couldn't pick her up.

TREATING HER ACURA AS A MEMBER OF THE FAMILY

Frances loved her little Acura Coupe, which she used often to go shopping. Now it was time to move again, so she wanted to sell the Acura, but not just to anyone. She had a nephew in Ames, Iowa who worked for the John Deere Corporation as a manager. He heard about the sale of the Acura and wanted to purchase the car badly. So she sold her nephew the vehicle. He loved the car and still has it in his possession to this day.

SHOPPING STYLES

In Bend, Oregon, Frances' shopping practices were highly revealed on a weekly basis. She would scan the newspaper for ads and coupons, and I would take her to at least four main stores to get the bargains that were advertised. In some cases, I would accompany her into the store and have to look at the lowest shelf for the right weight of the item that fit the coupon.

She sent me out one time to do the shopping and I was completely frustrated by not having the exact item that was in the coupon as I tried to check out. At one of these frustrating moments, I was sent by one of the cashiers to the customer service desk. It was a Friday night and there was a long line of people buying lottery tickets. I complained to the manager that there were mothers in this line with young children. I said it was against the law to have juveniles in the line where you are purchasing lottery tickets. So I told him in a joking manner, "You need to set up another line for customer service." This man bought the idea that I sold to him. So I was first in line.

CHAPTER 5

A Beautiful Lady

"How beautiful on the mountains are the feet of those who bring good news, who proclaim peace, who bring good tidings, who proclaim salvation, who say to Zion, "Your God Reigns!"

ISAIAH 52:7

Frances used very little or no makeup, since she was healthy and had natural beauty. Over the seven years she was treated for cancer, the doctor would comment how healthy she appeared, even though she was very sick with cancer.

Toward the end, the doctor wanted to know why she was so weak, so he ordered a spinal tap to see if cancer could be detected in her spinal fluid. She went into the examination room in a wheelchair and a nurse had to take a medical history of her treatment and put it in the computer. Frances knew all the names of the drugs and the chemicals she had taken and the several operations and the radiation treatments she had gone through. It took about 30 minutes for the nurse to record all this information from a very weak and sick woman. After the spinal tap, she was back in the wheelchair. I opened the doors to the hall at the hospital and there assembled in a semi-circle were the nurses and staff that the nurse who took the medical history had told about this amazing woman that was so beautiful, radiant and bright, despite years of treatment for cancer. I stopped so they could talk to Frances and tell her that they had heard how amazing and beautiful she was, and that they wanted to meet her.

On three occasions I had to call 911 to have the emergency service come and lift Frances off the floor. She would get out of bed and try to get to the bathroom and would fall down. On the last incident, she fell at the foot of the bed and it took four firemen to lift her into the bed safely. After they had spent some time checking her out for injuries and vital signs, they came out of the room and met me in the foyer to report on her condition before they left. The leader of the firemen said, "You sure have a beautiful wife." I agreed and said she is beautiful both inside and out.

FRANCES STYLED HER OWN HAIR

When I was dating Frances, I realized that she gave a lot of attention to how her hair looked. She very seldom went to a hairdresser. When she did go, she had to redo what had been done to make her hair look beautiful again. On one occasion, my daughters wanted to do something special for her and take her to one of the finest hair salons in the Seattle area. After I sat in the waiting room for some time looking through some of the magazines featuring various hairdos, Frances came out to show me the results. My first impression was that they had not finished and this was a chance for me to see the makeover in process. But I was told that this was it and she was ready to go. I said, "Didn't they show you some pictures of hairdos?" Anyway, she was able to remake this expensive makeover incorporating her own sense of beauty.

Frances shows-off her redo hairstyle.

LOVELY HATS FOR A BEAUTIFUL LADY

In the South, ladies often wore hats to go shopping and to church. It was all part of the Southern Belle charm. When we got married, I realized that Frances loved to dress up in beautiful hats. The thing is she was a beautiful lady in almost any hat. She could have been a model for advertising hats. She received many compliments when she wore a hat out anywhere. She actually bought hats before we could afford them. It was hard to deny a hat for a beautiful woman.

While living in Shaker Heights, Ohio we were just a city block away from the high school. We knew they had a very outstanding theater club that performed many classical plays. Frances realized they could use some of her dozen hats, so she donated some of them to the theater club. They used them to portray old-fashioned images.

CHARMING MRS. CASE

In Milwaukee, we had purchased a home owned by the Case family. The Cases were a wealthy family, and the Case name was well-known as a manufacturer of farm implements. After we bought the Case house, Frances and Mrs. Case became the best of friends. Frances was invited by Mrs. Case to go to the University Club for formal luncheons and dinners. Over the years, this was a wonderful outing for Frances. She was able to meet and know some of the elite women of Milwaukee. In other words, Mrs. Case was charmed by Frances and was anxious to get her young and beautiful friend known to others.

A RIDE IN A HORSE AND BUGGY

On a beautiful fall day in Leetonia, Ohio we decided to take a tour of the countryside to observe and appreciate the fall colors. Growing up in the South, Frances had never seen such a dramatic

Frances dresses up in a flowery hat for Easter Sunday

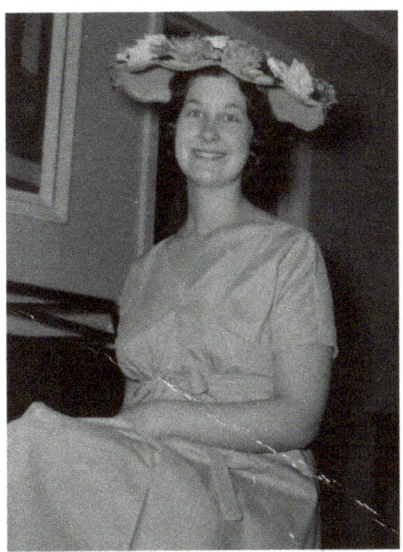

display of yellows, reds and browns. She took her sketch book along to record some oak trees, and several varieties of maple trees. In our tour, we were approached by an Amish man in a horse and buggy. Frances asked if she could take a ride, which would clearly be a new and dramatic experience. He accommodated her and took her on a short tour of the countryside.

CHAPTER 6

Very Intelligent and Bright

"His name was Nabal and his wife's name was Abigail. She was an intelligent and beautiful woman."
1 SAMUEL 25:3A

Frances was noted as an exceptional student in school by getting good grades. In some respects, she thought maybe she was the teacher's pet in grade school, since she was given special assignments and attention. In high school, she won a number of awards in her club activities, and again received excellent grades. When girls were thought not able to take chemistry, she was enrolled in the class and received the first and only A+ that had ever been given because she got all the answers correct on all the tests and examinations.

SECRETARY TO A JUVENILE JUDGE IN COLUMBUS, GEORGIA

Frances was an outstanding student in high school and was part of a program called Diversified Cooperative Training. Since the teaching staff knew she was very bright and capable, they assigned her to the juvenile court judge of the county on a half-day basis in her senior year. She was a very skilled and accomplished secretary.

Because Frances was such a beautiful and intelligent woman, she was never turned down for a job.

She could take shorthand, type nearly 100 words a minute, and was very proficient with the English language. She would take dictation of cases from the judge. He was very elderly and he would go to sleep in the easy chair while she would type up the cases. When she was finished with several cases, he would wake up, and she would share the typing with him and make any corrections. He was very satisfied with her work and wanted to keep her on a full-time basis after she graduated high school, but she had other plans.

TREASURER FOR DAYTONA BEACH COMMERCIAL CREDIT CORPORATION

Upon graduating from high school, Frances moved from Columbus, Georgia to Daytona Beach, Florida where she took a full-time job as treasurer for the Commercial Credit Corporation.

In other words, she was responsible for all the financial transactions for this thriving loan company. They had great confidence in her and wanted to keep her on until she retired. However, we decided to get married at the First Baptist Church in Daytona Beach, Florida, and she had to move to Leetonia, Ohio, which was so small it didn't even have a bank. So she applied at a small town south of Leetonia , where she was hired on at a bank. She was so talented, poised and beautiful, she had no trouble getting hired.

EXPERIENCE WITH MANPOWER, INCORPORATED

In Milwaukee, I was personally acquainted with Mr. Winters, the owner and CEO of Manpower Incorporated. I found out, in visits to Europe, that it was a worldwide agency for temporary employment. I saw a Manpower sign in every major city I visited. So, early on in our marriage, we moved around a lot. I was also working on my Ph.D. at Ohio State University. Although I was there for only the summer session, Frances applied for a short-term job with Manpower. She also would type papers I wrote in the graduate courses, which helped me get good grades.

Since I was personally acquainted with Mr. Winters, he told me that, as a boy, he never had a bar mitzvah. So he arranged to take his family to Israel so he could have a bar mitzvah at the Western Wall in Jerusalem. The women in his family were feminists and believed they should have equal opportunity. At the Western Wall, there were rules, one of which was that men and women couldn't sit at the same table together. Somehow he arranged to get the tables together to satisfy the women in his family. Frances and I had been at the Western Wall and witnessed bar mitzvah, weddings and celebrations. The men brought the trays around filled with delicacies to share with everyone, so we celebrated them as well.

She took a trip with Michelle to China and very quickly learned some Mandarin Chinese.

In preparation for the trip to Israel she reviewed the places we were visiting with the study of the Bible and the many reference books in her library.

Dr. Boone, her oncologist, told me that she was one of the brightest patients that he had ever had. She was always prepared with pertinent questions for each appointment and had background on all the chemo treatments that she was receiving. She had me research on the internet the makeup of the drugs and chemicals and their effects.

GOOD AT ROLLER SKATING

Frances enjoyed roller skating. Every weekend, when she was in high school, she would go to a USO sponsored skating event at Fort Benning, Georgia which included soldiers. She told me a young solder from Long island, NY was her partner every week. Eventually he told her that when she grew up he would like to marry her. She was about 16 then. When we got married she wanted me to go skating with her. I had never roller skated at a rink, so she had to hold me up at times. She got tired of doing that. We never went roller skating again.

RUNNING RACES AND KEEPING UP WITH THE CHILDREN

Frances loved a contest. So when the children were growing up, she would footrace them to the end of the driveway, and then to the corner of the block. She liked to win every race, and could usually win a footrace.

My granddaughter, who was trained at the high school level to do competitive swimming, came to Bend, Oregon for a summer visit. We took her to the city aquatic center, which had an Olympic size pool. Bethany was showing off her new swimming skills, since she was on the swim team at her high school. I told Frances and Bethany, "Why don't you two swim to the end of the pool and see who gets there first." So Bethany took up the challenge and they dove off the side of the pool. Bethany knew she could win against her grandmother. Frances dove under the water like a porpoise and swam most of the distance under water. She came out the other end a body length ahead of Bethany. She loved a contest and would take on a challenge.

Another event was funny. Frances' sister and her husband came from Florida and we went out for a picnic and played football. Frances was a member of the line and went against her brother-in-law on the other side. She was holding her own but the brother-in-law played a trick on her. When she ran forward, he got out of the way and Frances landed flat on the ground. She wasn't afraid to take a risk.

FIRE IN GROVE CITY, OHIO

Since Frances grew up in the South, she was not familiar with the various means to keep the house warm during severe winter weather. In the Grove City, Ohio home, we had a beautiful and elaborate fireplace. At Christmas time, I built a fire in the fireplace to provide warmth and cheer during the holiday season.

I went off to work one morning and Frances decided to clean out the ashes. She put them in a cardboard box and took it to the garage. My daughter Michelle, about two years old, was crawling up the steps from the basement and said, "I smell smoke." Smoke was coming out under the door to the garage. Frances opened the door to the garage and found flames going up the wall from the cardboard box. She quickly grabbed a bucket of water and rushed to put out the fire. The garage contained a large number of flammables. Without the alarm from Michelle, the house would have caught fire. Frances learned to put ashes in metal containers. She didn't know there were live coals in the ashes.

RAISING A LITTER OF DOBERMANS

Frances' good friend Marjorie, who now lived in South Carolina, had a litter of pups from her Doberman. So on our trip back from Florida we stopped and brought home a Doberman puppy. She named her Queenie and trained our puppy so she could stay in our home. Queenie was a very good dog. She slept on our first step to the basement. When I told her to go to the basement, she proceeded downstairs, where she would go for the evening and to rest. This command came in handy when we went on our camping trips. We had a family size tent and she had a pup tent of her own to sleep in. I would tell her, "Go to the basement," and she would go into her tiny pup tent and sleep there all night.

Frances learned as much as she could about Doberman dogs. In some respects, she became an expert. She took Queenie, our Doberman, to a breeder and she finally delivered nine puppies. Frances read books to understand the birthing process. We both watched the birth of the puppies. Without reading the book, Queenie did everything during the birthing process naturally. It was as if she had read the book and knew exactly what to do.

They were all born blind and completely helpless. Queenie was a devoted mom. She never wanted to leave her puppies for even a minute. She would go outside to do her duty and make a great grand circle, and then return inside to her puppies. Most Dobermans are black, but two were brown. And one of the brown ones was a huge dog.

There was a lot of cleanup for nine puppies and we used a lot of newspapers to train them. The soiled newspapers were put in a permanent incinerator. It was quite a convenient way to get rid of the soiled newspaper mess.

We had a piece of plywood over the laundry tubs to groom them. Frances would put them in a stance that was required in a dog show. The dogs received their vaccinations; we had their ears and tails trimmed as well. The only one that the tail and ear trimming didn't affect was the runt of the litter. He was known as Little

Frances poses with Oscar, our largest Doberman.

Bit. He continually tried to keep licking his tail so we had to put a cone collar on him. He looked like an elephant with big ears. When he was first born, he was so tiny and weak that I fed him through a Barbie doll milk bottle.

  I continually followed all of the procedures that Queenie had for her puppies. Frances didn't advertise, but somehow received a phone call from a Chicago dog owner. He asked for the most dominant male dog. Frances sold him for $500 and we shipped him off to the gentleman. He was so pleased with the male puppy that he then wanted the most dominant female puppy. So for $500, Frances shipped our most dominant female puppy off to Chicago as well. She sold many of our other dogs to owners who did dog shows, and many of our puppies went on to win blue ribbons.

Frances took care of all these pups like they were her own babies. She kept them nicely groomed and had their nails trimmed. Frances learned how to train them, so many of them became show dogs and won blue ribbons. She made a lot of money on them. We had Queenie for about 10 years.

There was one dog that was huge. We called him Oscar. He thought he was a lap dog and would run up into your lap and think he was the smallest dog ever. But he was definitely the biggest dog. One day, Oscar ran out into the road and a small car hit him. The owner said he put a dent in the vehicle. Yet Oscar wasn't even hurt; he was fine. Frances finally sold Oscar.

The last dog we had to sell was Little Bit. A farmer in Iowa wanted a Doberman so Frances gave him glowing reports on Little Bit. Frances cried a little bit but she sold him at a good price. The farmer called back after he had Little Bit for quite a while, and said that he was the best dog he has had on his farm. He was very pleased with Little Bit.

COLLECTING HER SOCIAL SECURITY

Frances knew how to handle a dollar. She was a very frugal shopper and watched every penny she spent. When she turned 63, she asked the IRS about her account. I went to Social Security to check on my account and the agent said, "Your wife can begin getting a check when she is 63. She could get $203 a month." Frances had been a homemaker most of the time, and was never employed over a long period of time. So she didn't collect much from Social Security. She began to get a check for $203 every month, which she viewed as her own money. She asked me to set up a separate bank account so she could build it up and watch her money grow. She never spent the money.

CHAPTER 7

Born in a One Room Cabin to Become a World Traveler

> "[The Church in Antioch] Now those who had been scattered by the persecution that broke out when Stephen was killed traveled as far as Phoenicia, Cyprus and Antioch, spreading the word only among Jews."
> ACTS 11:19

Frances was born in a one room cabin on a farm in southern Georgia. The cabin was constructed of pine tree planks with space between them, so that chickens could be seen under the floor. In the winter time, cold air would come through the cracks in the walls

The Funderburk brothers came to Georgia from South Carolina carrying only a knapsack. They went to work at a farm house and eventually married the farmer's daughters. This way they inherited some farm land and got off to a good start. One of the brothers was Frances' grandfather. Unfortunately, the men in the Funderburk family were alcoholics and would get drunk on weekends and beyond. So Frances' mother had to leave Georgia and go back to Florida. This is where Frances lived her earlier years. Most of the time it was during World War II.

Her father, who was an alcoholic, began attending a country Baptist Church and gave his life to the Lord. His salvation was a complete beginning. He was now a new creature and gave up alcohol for the rest of his life. He was a very pleasant and wonderful man to know. We had many conversations when we'd visit the farm house in Georgia.

Progress came slowly on the Georgia farms that her father owned. You could follow the gradual progress if you followed the development of running water. The first water was furnished to the hogs across the road from the newly built farm house. The next development was to bring it across the road to a tank holding water near the new house. The next move was to bring it into the kitchen so there would be running water. However, they kept the open well using buckets to bring in the fresh water. Finally, a bathroom was added to the farm house for the last step in the process. Before these developments, water was used in the fields to irrigate the tobacco crops. So much for progress. The farm house took years to develop.

BOUGHT HER OWN PIANO

Frances went to work in a theater when she was 14. She had many tasks, but basically was selling popcorn. She saved her money and bought a new piano, a Baldwin upright. And she paid for her own piano lessons. She learned to play the classics, plus hymns of the church. She was so different from other members of her family and brought classical music into that environment.

After we were married at the Daytona Beach First Baptist Church, we loaded the piano in a U-Haul trailer and brought it all the way back to Leetonia, Ohio. It was a prized possession and centerpiece in our duplex.

Later on, Frances gave the Baldwin away so the grandsons could learn to play the piano. I bought her a Steinway baby grand in Cleveland Ohio, so the quality of the piano would match her love for music. It cost $36,000. We immediately moved to Bend, Oregon and the movers were bonded and experts in moving a valuable piano. Once they moved the piano on a skid into the music library room, they took it off the skid and it dropped. I heard the piano play, but it wasn't damaged. Another man, all by himself, moved the piano from Bend to my second home in Covington, Washington and he did everything by himself. He said the piano had grown in value because Steinway makes only a limited number. So the longer you keep the piano, the more valuable it becomes.

WASHING DISHES IN THE TOLEDO HOME

Many of the homes we bought in the Midwest were old and didn't have any automatic dishwashers. A little girl was visiting Frances in the kitchen. As Frances was washing dishes in the sink, the little girl asked if she could watch her. She said she had never seen anyone washing dishes and this was a fascinating experience for her. Her homes always had dishwashers, so this was a first for her.

World Travels

ENTRANCE TO THE CITY OF JERUSALEM

I was invited to go to Israel to negotiate a contract to exchange high school students with major cities in America. Frances went with me as a companion but, more importantly, as a student of the Bible and out of a great love for the Jewish People. Before our trip, Frances studied the Bible, and did research on all of the cities we were to visit. We were traveling from Tel Aviv through the mountains to Jerusalem on a tour bus. Frances and I had the very front seats, so we were able to get a terrific view through the front windshield. We came over the mountain into Jerusalem in the evening hour. The evening sun was shining on the Jerusalem stone, making the city look like the "City of Gold." Frances said this clearly so everyone on the bus could hear her. She said, "That is the Shakina glory." In the Bible, that is a reference to God's presence with the people of Israel. For Frances, that was a glorious revelation, to see Jerusalem in that light.

We walked the streets that Jesus walked. The archeologists dug down three layers that were common during the Roman's rule of Israel. The street was filled with arched doors that indicated it was a shopping area filled with small shops. The floor of the street was made of white marble tiles, and there was a sewer system for the water to run off. The city was not as primitive as one would think. Also, in the center of the street were statues of Roman rulers. The phrase "removing the head of state" took on a whole new meaning. When there were new Roman rulers, they didn't replace the statue – they replaced only the head.

The Roman Empire was thought to be cruel and overwhelming by enslaving many people in the known world. But in many respects, they brought many advances to the known world, such as Roman law, providing justice in the court system, aqueducts, irrigation, beautiful columns and arched architectural structures. Even in Israel, the synagogues reflected the Roman architecture. In a city like Capernaum, the relics from the synagogues had Roman columns. Also in the ruins, I found the Star of David carved in a stone.

In Capernaum, Saint Peter, the fisherman, launched his boats into the Sea of Galilee. The foundation of his home was visible until I returned on my second visit. I was shocked to see that the Catholic Church had built a store that sold relics over the original site that was so important.

The Romans loved recreation centers. They built Caesarea off the coast of the Mediterranean Sea so the rulers would have a safe place to go swimming and enjoy the water.

CONFERENCES IN BRUSSELS AND PARIS

I was also invited to a conference on education and economic development, which was part of NATO. Frances went with me, and we were in Brussels and Paris at conference sites. We made a side trip into Germany and took the train to West Berlin, going through East Germany. The overnight trip included several interruptions by soldiers with long guns and guard dogs. They searched every nook and corner of the train, including underneath the train. There were several stops on the route so there were numerous searches. In the morning, we were met by a German family that had visited us in Milwaukee. We were now in West Berlin, which was bustling with activity and had been rebuilt, with only one exception, which served as a reminder of the destruction that had taken place during the war.

We went through Checkpoint Charlie into another world, which was East Berlin. There were no goods being displayed and very little activity or traffic on the streets. The people we saw along the way wore the drab clothes issued to them, and the famous Pergamon Museum and the cathedral next to it had not been repaired from the destruction of WWII. However, the archeological displays at the Pergamon Museum were amazing. Berlin's Pergamon Museum is known for its imposing reconstruction of the Ishtar Gate from Babylon, the ancient Mesopotamian city in what is today, Iraq. Also, the first gate to the walled city of Babylon, the hanging gardens and the turquoise blue tiles on the way into Babylon with large figures of lions, were spectacular and left a lasting impression on Frances. She had studied the story of Daniel and wondered how he felt, coming as a Jewish slave boy into an enormous and beautiful city rising up out of the desert.

TRAIN TRIP THROUGH SPAIN

In order to get to Brussels, Belgium to meet the NATO authorities, we had to take a fast train through Spain, which was loaded with labor union leaders heading to a convention. So we had some very interesting conversations.

TRIP TO GREAT BRITAIN

In order to get some relief from the pressures of my job, Frances and I were planning a trip to visit Ireland. However, something important had come up to which I had to give attention. But I still wanted Frances to go on the trip which she had put so much effort into planning. So I called my daughters Michelle and Marianne to see if they could accommodate her on this trip. My daughters agreed to go. They took a plane from New York to Shannon, Ireland, hired a rental car and began their two week adventure around Great Britain. Frances was reported to be a good traveler, even though she was loaded down much of the time with a heavy backpack. They took in all the sights of Ireland, England, and Wales, sleeping overnight in many different hostels to cut down on expenses. They took many pictures, as well as many videos, which demonstrated Frances was a very happy traveler.

A TRIP TO EUROPE

My brother Roger, who was the Minister of Music at the Coral Ridge Presbyterian Church in Fort Lauderdale, Florida wanted to arrange a tour to Europe for his choir. He invited Frances and me to go with him, so we joined him, traveling throughout Europe, visiting prominent cathedrals in which he was scheduling his choir to perform. We traveled throughout Europe in a Mercedes Benz, which he eventually bought and had shipped to the US. The

Frances visits Germany during the winter, posing next to historic monuments.

cathedrals were very old and ornate; some of them had taken 100 years to construct. Several generations of a family would be a part of this construction.

A TRIP TO ALASKA

When I was 70 years old, Frances and I made arrangements for 13 family members to take a cruise on a ship from Seattle, Washington to Alaska. This was the first of several cruises our family would take together. We visited all the ports of Alaska. The one that was particularly exciting was the visit to Juneau, the capital of Alaska. This was actually a revisit since I had been there many years ago when visiting the pastor of the Methodist Church in Grove City, Ohio. After several days on the trip, Frances noticed a woman who appeared to be the pastor's wife. We went to the registration desk to see if he and his wife were on board. It appeared that they were on board, as well with their own grown family and grandchildren. We began looking for them and opened the door to the deck. There was the pastor taking a walk around the ship on the deck. He was so surprised! Then we got our families together and took pictures commemorating the chance meeting.

TRIP TO CANADA

We took a vacation trip with the entire family and our Doberman, Queenie, and visited Canada. One of the highlights were the Thousand Islands. We found out that Kate Smith actually owned one of these private islands. We had no problem getting Queenie into Canada. But on our return to the US, the customs officials wouldn't let Queenie back into the United States without her papers. Leaving Queenie in Canada was not an option for my children. So all three began sobbing and crying hysterically, which played on the sympathies of the customs officials. Queenie was eventually allowed to come back into the States without any papers.

RESCUE TRIP TO NEBRASKA

My family had many experiences with the Chinese, since my daughter took Mandarin Chinese in high school. She kept up with any new family that came to Milwaukee. In addition, from time to time, we would house international couples in our third floor apartment. We had a lady from mainland China who came to the U.S. to obtain her Ph.D. in economics at the University of Wisconsin-Milwaukee. She brought her husband, daughter and a baby with her, so we were very well acquainted with the family.

This family was unique. The wife was trained by the Communists and spoke fluent Russian, as well as Mandarin Chinese. The daughter may have been about five years old and the boy was just a baby. Frances questioned the way they supervised their children; they

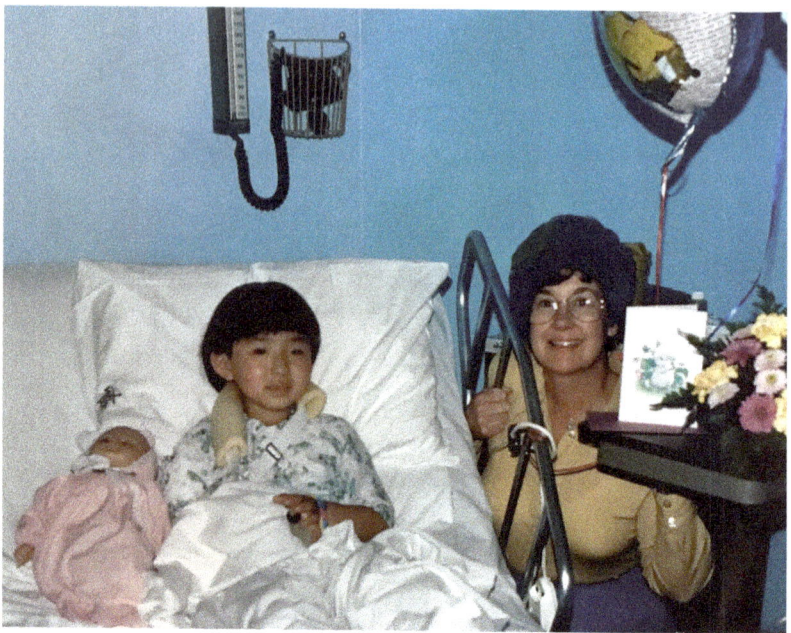

Frances to the rescue.

gave them lots of freedom to explore. We learned some norms for raising children in a Chinese family. The babies were allowed to crawl or roam around at night while the parents were in bed. Rooms were baby safe. Discipline didn't apply until they were age five and able to go to school.

The husband was looking for a job, and received an offer in California. The family had to move from Milwaukee all the way across the United States. In the flatlands of Nebraska, they stopped across the street from a market and the little girl misunderstood the speed of the cars that were going 40 miles per hour on a highway. They had always lived in major urban centers, so she tried to cross the street as if she was in a city. The driver tried to stop when he saw her crossing the road, but she ran into the boat he was hauling and was knocked to the ground, suffering very severe injuries. She was taken to the county hospital.

Her mother notified Frances about the accident and Frances

Frances' sister Betty Jean and her husband Mason.

Creativity on the Beach.

understood how helpless they would be, so she immediately flew to Scottsbluff, Nebraska and went directly to the hospital. There she met a nurse who was providing housing to the Chinese family, and the nurse invited Frances to accompany her at her home. Frances stayed with the family until the little girl was discharged from the hospital, and the family continued their travels to California. On one of our vacation trips to the Western U.S., we stopped in Nebraska to visit this wonderful Christian nurse to show our appreciation for her hospitality.

TRIPS TO FLORIDA

We took many trips from the northland to Florida to visit Frances' family. We often tried to drive straight through. Frances wanted me to get a little relief while we were going through the mountain passes in West Virginia. So I was now in the passenger seat, closing my eyes to get some rest. I opened my eyes briefly and saw that the headlights were off. It scared me because Frances was driving at night through the mountains with no headlights. I asked her what was wrong and she said, "I turned the headlights off to scare myself so I wouldn't go to sleep." On another occasion in the winter time, Frances opened the window so she could stay awake. This was a little less dangerous than turning the lights off.

SEVERAL TRIPS TO ARIZONA

We took several trips from the northland to Phoenix, Arizona. It would generally take three days to get there. On one of these trips through the state of Utah, you could travel very fast down the state highways, which were very straight. You could see miles ahead of you without traffic. Sometimes you couldn't even get one radio station. On one of these long stretches, Frances wanted to drive. In order to be completely safe, even during the day, I wanted to turn the headlights on. In fumbling around, I must have touched

Frances took a ride on a ricksha in Taiwan.

the button for kilometers, because Frances saw we were going over 100 miles per hour. I explained to her that I must have touched the wrong button, so wasn't really going over 100 miles per hour. Her response was, "It certainly didn't feel like it."

TRIP TO CHINA

My daughter, Michelle, took Mandarin Chinese for two years in high school. Sadly, it was not offered at University of Wisconsin-Milwaukee. So I promised Michelle that she could go to Taiwan to spend time refining her new language. Upon graduation, she flew out of Chicago and spent nearly four years in Taiwan. At the American International School, she gave private piano lessons and English tutoring to the children of rich families. Doing this, she was able to support herself living in an apartment building, which also had many other challenges. There were flying roaches, and large spiders in the shower stall. Outside her apartment window there was a large mountain of garbage, which attracted rodents.

Michelle invited Frances to visit her in Taiwan. She took Frances on tours of the island, visiting small fishing villages where she visited homes. The homes sometimes served her with small guppy-sized fish swimming around in the soup.

Michelle then took her mother to Hong Kong, then on into mainland China. They rode the buses in Hong Kong and, over the years, I told Frances that the yellow school buses were nearly worn out. They were sold to churches to transport children to Sunday school. When I visited Mexico, I told Frances that the buses were then sold to companies in Mexico. She told me that the buses had their last days in Hong Kong. She could see the road go by under the bus, since the floor was nearly gone beneath her feet.

The grand trip was highlighted by a passenger train ride into mainland China from Hong Kong to Canton. They treated them both as college students since Frances looked so young, so they got discounts on their tickets. The train was very crowded, and people brought their live pigs and chickens aboard the train. The riders ate chicken legs and threw the remains on the floor. They also spit on the floor. She could not believe the filth on the train. She and Michelle had to stand most of the time, so they got a good view of what was happening.

After their visit to China, they came back to Taiwan to catch a plane back to the United States. The customs officials isolated Michelle for investigations for several hours, because she returned with tour guides for China. They thought she was bringing back documents from China. She was finally cleared, yet Frances had to suffer through this wait, not knowing exactly what would happen to an American in this foreign country.

Michelle was easily recognized in Taiwan by the local residents, since she appeared on a very popular dating show that was broadcast daily on nationwide television. So on the street she would be noticed for several reasons. One was exposure on this television show; another was she was a tall American woman. She could hear their conversations in Mandarin Chinese saying she was a "big American Barbie doll." Needless to say, Michelle and Frances returned to the States safe and sound.

CHAPTER 8

Providing Hospitality

"Do not forget to show hospitality to strangers,
for by so doing some people have shown hospitality
to angels without knowing it."

HEBREWS 13:2

INTERNATIONAL HOSPITALITY IN THE THIRD FLOOR APARTMENT

In the Milwaukee, Wisconsin home purchased from the Case family, there was a third floor apartment for housing the servants. Frances saw this as an opportunity to show Southern hospitality to international students. She was in constant contact with the International Student Department at the University of Wisconsin-Milwaukee. We showed hospitality to students from Malaysia, Singapore, Hong Kong, Taiwan and Egypt, and an extensive stay by a mainland Chinese family.

BOYS FROM SOMALIA

The most interesting visitors were two boys from Somalia who finished their high school years at Riverside High School in Milwaukee. Our local church had a special mission in Somalia, so we were quite acquainted with the needs of Somalians, such as providing clean water. One of the boys was tall and all African; the other boy was part Italian and very short. The boys told of all the experiences they had in Somalia. They played soccer on the sand beach using coconuts. They also saw the Russians leave with their soldiers and tanks loaded onto ships. The smaller boy came home from high school, saying they wanted him to join the football team. I asked him, "Do you mean the soccer team?" He responded and said, "No, American football." I thought he was very small and told him he shouldn't play football. After he put the uniform on, he looked at himself in the mirror and said, "I was very big." I said, "What did the coach want you to do?" He said, "He wanted me to kick the football, and told me to drop to the ground and cover my head so I wouldn't get hurt." He was very good at kicking the football.

Frances wanted the boys to learn how to do chores, so she asked them to mow the lawn. They had never seen grass lawns until they came to America. They also didn't know how to operate a lawn mower. So I watched them mow all around in circles, so I told them I had to teach them how to use it correctly.

The smaller boy's mother had an accident in Somalia and broke her shoulder. It was never repaired. Frances was the chair of the hospital visit committee at our church, and she knew the doctors. So she asked a doctor if he would treat this African mother. Frances invited his mother to come to Milwaukee to meet the finest surgeons around. They surgeons examined her shoulder and found, over the years, she had made some adjustments to using it. Repairing it would have been a difficult and painful procedure. The doctor examined her and said she would go through several years of painful operations to correct the injury. She had adjusted to life and could handle most activities, so he did not recommend surgery. After this, she went back to Somalia.

AN EGYPTIAN FAMILY

An Egyptian family occupied the apartment for a number of months while the wife was taking graduate courses in library science at the university. She said that Nasser, the prime minister of Egypt, sent them money every month to help support them. I looked at one of the checks- it was a US Treasury check. I looked at one of the payments so I thought this may be a part of a treaty with Egypt. So it may not have been just a special gift to this family.

FAMILY GUESTS

Frances loved to entertain family members who visited us. In several locations, her mother and step- father visited us and she made things very comfortable. On occasion her mother came alone. Once, in Milwaukee, she came to be with Frances during Christmas time. The weekends in the Christmas season were very cold, with temperatures very low at 30 below zero. Her mother, coming from Florida, had never experienced this frigid weather. She said she didn't mind looking outside and seeing the snow and the ice. But when there was frost on the windows and around the door casings, she said she was very frightened. She actually went home early and never came back again to our home in Milwaukee.

Frances' sister Betty Jean and her husband visited us a number of times at each of our new locations. They came back frequently in order to enjoy the hospitality and the local sights. In Milwaukee, Michelle, our daughter, was married in the local Methodist church. The reception after the wedding was in our back yard with a string quartet and several tables filled with goodies. On another occasion, Frances planned a celebration in our yard on my 50th birthday. Again, she set up the tables, which were highly decorated, and

Frances greets me with a kiss and a beautifully decorated 50th Birthday cake.

served lasagna with homemade bread and cheesecake for dessert. The guests were my immediate staff and their families and members of the school board. This was quite the undertaking. She did this almost single handedly.

AN EXAMPLE OF COUNSELING

There was a moment in the program at her funeral here in Bend in which members of the church and others could honor and fondly remember Frances. At the end of this moment in the program, a lady stood and walked toward the aisle and began relating a story that was a surprise to everyone. It was all hard to believe. She said that she had heard from a friend in Milwaukee, Wisconsin that Frances had passed away and that she could possibly go to her funeral. As a young lady, she had come to our home to talk to Frances after she had lost both of her parents and her brother in a serious auto accident. In her mind, life was over. How could she go on living without her family? She said that Frances listened and encouraged her not to quit, that she could do anything she put her mind to and could accomplish great things in life. These thoughts guided her through life, and she was so grateful to Frances who contributed so much to her future and wellbeing. The counseling took place nearly 35 years ago. The lady is now an administrator for the United Way in Bend, Oregon.

My daughters were surprised to see this lady, who they knew quite well during the high school years in Milwaukee. They recognized her after all these years and went to her and warmly embraced her.

CELEBRATING MY 50TH BIRTHDAY

Frances secretly planned a birthday celebration that took place in our beautiful yard in Milwaukee, Wisconsin. She invited about 50 members of my staff and served them a delicious meal and a beautifully decorated cake with fresh daisies.

CHAPTER 9

A Sincere Spiritual Life Growing Toward Maturity

"For this very reason, make every effort to add to your faith goodness; and to goodness, knowledge; and to knowledge, self-control; and to self-control, perseverance; and to perseverance, godliness; and to godliness, mutual affection; and to mutual affection, love."

2 PETER 1: 5-7

Frances had a long and maturing walk with the Lord. As a child, she attended a nearby small Baptist Church with an active Sunday school and devoted teachers. The teacher she fondly remembered was a man that nurtured her in the faith and led her to a saving grace with her Lord. She often looked back on this as her spiritual birth, which gave her new life, and with the Savior's guidance, help to protect her during these tender years.

In Milwaukee she was immersed in service to the Lord. At an inner city church, she taught fourth grade students in Sunday school each Sunday and was the leader of the Hospitality Committee, where she had to totally plan and deliver dinners for special occasions. She was also the contact person in charge of calling on the sick and assisting families that were in crisis.

She hosted organized youth groups at our home for devotions, Bible study and song fests. She also had the Chosen People, a

Christian Jewish organization meet at our home for study and leadership training. She became very devoted to the Jewish People and the nation of Israel.

She met weekly with an elderly retired school teacher who was very interested in Bible study and Christian fellowship. She was a resident of the Methodist Home.

Frances studied the Bible extensively with great intensity. She had several Bibles and each has pages full of notations, which helped her gain meaning and provide a point of reference for further research. She built a library full of reference books, which she could access to answer questions from her inquisitive mind or those questions coming from relatives and friends. Those questions never went unanswered; she always did some research.

She was indeed a student of the Bible. In Milwaukee, she took several Bible classes from the Moody Bible Institute Extension School. She wrote excellent papers and received several certificates of achievement. From the comments of her professors on the work she did, it appeared that she was most likely one of their finest students.

She was faithful in listening to her favorite radio pastors and expositors of the Word. She tape recorded many of these messages so that she could play them over again, as well as share them with others.

Godly counseling was one of her most valuable contributions to the lives of many in her family and beyond. She had sensitivity to others and was an intelligent listener. But she did not take on this task of service to the Lord lightly. She took several courses on Christian Counseling and continued to be a student of Christian Counseling by reading extensively on the subject.

A PRAYER WARRIOR AND A PETITIONER

Regardless of the situation or occasion, Frances' prayers were carefully structured and you knew she was praying to her Heavenly Father. Written prayers found in her Bible, which were for the family, the church, and the world, could be prayed today and still are pertinent and have great meaning.

There is no end to the precious attributes of Frances. I keep remembering many, and there are more that come to mind the longer I live. But I want to share this much with you after nine years of precious memories.

www.ingramcontent.com/pod-product-compliance
Lightning Source LLC
Chambersburg PA
CBHW062104290426
44110CB00022B/2707